Evening at the Met

A Visit to the Museum of Art

Plate 2

An Evening at the Theater

Tea in the Garden

Plate 8

Promenade on the Avenue

Awaiting the Arrival of Relatives from Connecticut

A Train Trip to Boston

Holidays Uptown

A Walk Down the Aisle

Plate 16